WHAT IS WONDERLAND CAFE...?

Internet cafes, or cybercafes, are places that have computers available, usually for a fee, that you can use to go online. Internet cafes can be set up in actual eating/drinking establishments, cruise ships, or other types of locations.

Wonderland - A fictional country

Wonderland Cafe - A fictional cafe that exists in the mind and on the web. A place that brings together all the coolest stuff that geek culture has to offer.

Forever Hatter

Tea Party Cookbook

Designed by
Buffy Naillon

In conjunction with

FORVER HATTER: MAD TEA PARTY COOKBOOK

THESE AIN'T NO CONFIDENTIAL, TOP-SECRET RECIPES FROM LITERARY KITCHENS KINDA COOKBOOKS SERIES

A publication of Cinder Apple Press, Wonderland Cafe, and Buffy Naillon.

None of this work may be transmitted or reproduced in any form -- electronic, mechanical, printed, translated or stored as information or via electronic retrieval system without the permission of the author except where copyright law allows for review purposes or for educational use. You may not re-upload and resell this book for distribution to others.

Cover Design: Buffy Naillon
Illustrations: Buffy Naillon, John Tenniel
Interior Design: Buffy Naillon
Source materials: Modified images from Open Clip Art, Alice in Wonderland Public domain

ISBN-13: 978-1542470766
ISBN-10: 1542470765

...SSIBLE TH...
...CAPTAIN ALICE AT T...
...DREAMED OF IMPOSS...
...DE THEM...
...THEN...
...THINGS...
...IMP...
...SIBLE...
...ING IS...
...GATING IMPOSSIBLE...
...YING THE JABBERWO...
...KING BETTER TEA TH...
...ALL TH...

Simple Marmalade

Ingredients:

1 Medium navel orange
2 Tablespoons water
1/2 c. Sugar

Simple Marmalade, Cont.

Instructions:

Select navel oranges that have the thinnest peel.

If the orange is large double the amount of water and sugar.

> Wash the orange thoroughly.
>
> Cut off both ends of the orange.

Cut the orange in half, cut each half in about eight sections.

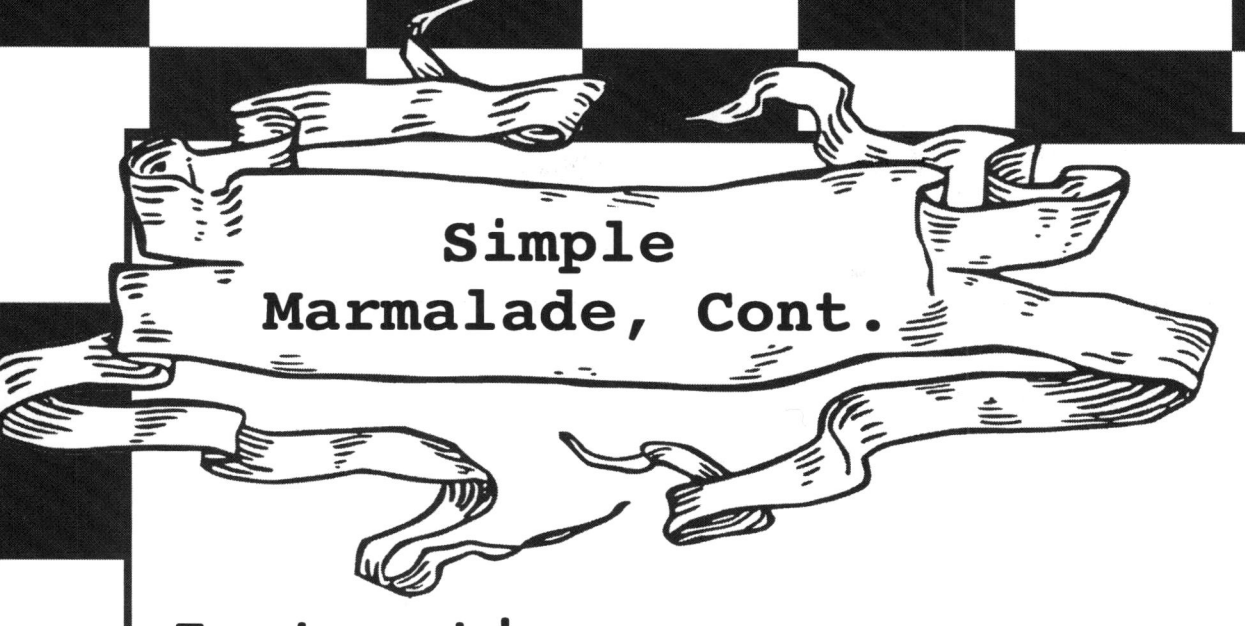

Simple Marmalade, Cont.

Instructions:

Place the orange sections in the food processor and pulse until the peel in is tiny pieces.

In a medium saucepan place the processed orange, the water and the sugar and bring to a gentle boil.

Boil for 15 minutes, stirring frequently.

Let cool, then place in a glass jar with a tight fitting lid.

Refrigerate to store.

When it is cold it is ready to eat.

About Low Tea...

From "Alice's Adventures in Wonderland: Food in Literature Edition"

"Low tea, on the other hand, started at the 4:00 o'clock hour, included mostly women at first, and was served on low chairs or tables like coffee tables, thus the name. It's the kind of tea you think of when you remember passages from books written by Jane Austen.

Bread and butter, biscuits, crust-less sandwiches, hot buttered scones, and cake counted as the fare at low tea, much like they did at the Hatter's tea party."

The Un-Rules of High Tea

Did you know...

"Despite its name, high tea actually originated with the lower classes. Dinner was served midday in the 1800s, but in practice, working stiffs didn't have the luxury of an afternoon lunch break, so they took tea right after work with heartier fare — like pies, meats and cheeses — to sate their hunger.

Richardson says the name high tea probably evolved from the fact that this evening meal was served at proper dinner tables, rather than on couches or settees. Using the term 'high tea' when you really mean 'afternoon tea' is a dead giveaway you're American."
Quote source: NPR

YEP!

High tea is really like eating lunch in a roadside diner...

Not Suitable for vegetarians

The Un-Rules for Tea Parties

According to the BBC...

There aren't any rules when it comes to the food, but a standard afternoon tea comprises a layer of sandwiches, a layer of cakes and a layer of scones or teacakes.

However, you could also throw in pastries, petits fours or biscuits.

Mocha Java Cont.

Ingredients:

2 c. Milk
2 TBSP Cocoa mix
2 TBSP Brown sugar
1 TBSP Ground coffee
1 tsp Vanilla extract
Sprinkle of cinnamon, optional
Sprinkle of cayenne pepper, optional

Instructions:

Heat up the ingredients in a saucepan.

Strain it and then pour into 2 coffee mugs.

Add cinnamon or cayenne pepper for some extra zest!

Tea Party Lemonade

Ingredients:

1 3/4 White sugar
8 c. Water
1 1/2 c. Lemon juice

Instructions:

Take one cup of the water.

Add it and the sugars to a saucepan. Bring this to a boil.

Pour into a pitcher. Store in the fridge.

Stir the lemon juice with the pulp into the chilled syrup. Add the rest of the water.

Fun Tip...
Add a dash of vanilla for extra flavor!

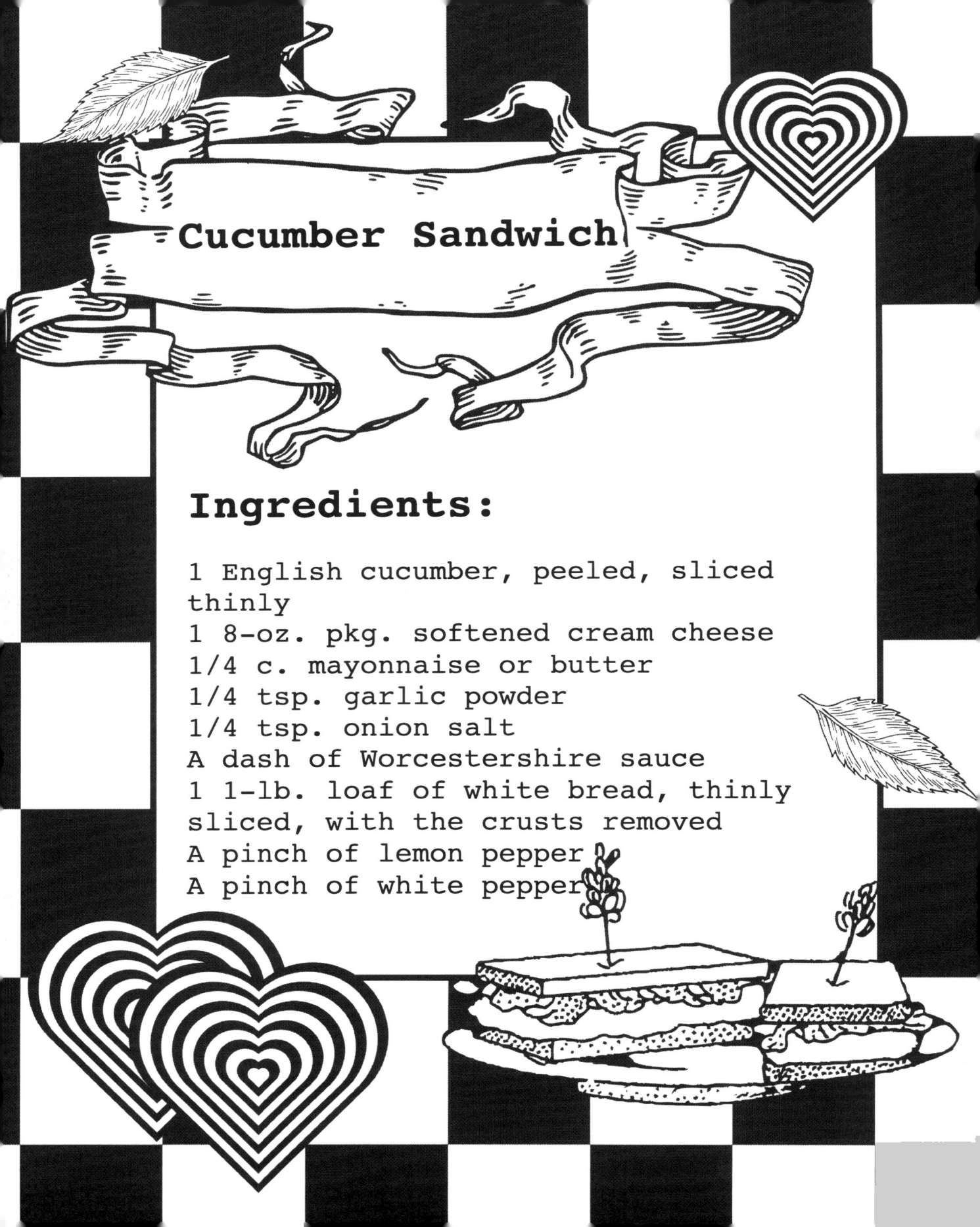

Cucumber Sandwich

Ingredients:

1 English cucumber, peeled, sliced thinly
1 8-oz. pkg. softened cream cheese
1/4 c. mayonnaise or butter
1/4 tsp. garlic powder
1/4 tsp. onion salt
A dash of Worcestershire sauce
1 1-lb. loaf of white bread, thinly sliced, with the crusts removed
A pinch of lemon pepper
A pinch of white pepper

Cucumber Sandwich, Cont.

Instructions:

Drain the cucumber slices in a colander. To do this, place two paper towels in the colander, with the cuke slices between each sheet. Let them sit for 10 minutes or so.

Mix together the mayo, cream cheese, onion salt, garlic powder, and Worcestershire sauce in a bowl until smooth.

If you prefer butter to mayo, substitute that. Make sure it's room temperature.

Tea Party Egg Salad

Tips...

Using older eggs, as well as seasoning the water with salt and vinegar, will make for easy peeling.
...Food and Wine

Ingredients:

1 halved, seeded and peeled Hass Avocado (make sure it's ripe)

6 peeled and halved hard-boiled eggs

1 Tbsp white wine vinegar

1 tsp Dijon mustard

½ tsp salt

½ c. minced onion

2 Tbsp chopped chives

Instructions:

Take the yolks out of two of the eggs. Chop up the rest of the whites and the rest of the yolks and set aside.

In a separate bowl, combine the mustard, avocado, vinegar and salt. Mash these ingredients until the mixture becomes smooth.

Dice up the rest of the avocados and add them to the mixture.

Add in the onions and eggs as well, mixing them together gently.

Tea Party Egg Salad, Cont

Ham Salad, Cont.

Ingredients:

1 1/2 lbs Chopped, cooked ham
1/2 to 3/4 c. Mayo
1/3 c. Minced onions, dried
1/3 c. Pickle relish
1/4 c. Brown mustard
2 TBSP Garlic powder, optional

Instructions:

Chop up the ham in a food processor. Be careful not to chop it up so much it becomes pasty-like.

Mix the rest of the ingredients together.

Serve on your choice of bread. Cut into samll pieces.

Meet Our Cook

Salad
We don't believe in it... But we do serve dressing by the jar...

Menu

Now Serving:
High Tea at

The WONDERLAND CAFE

Asparagus Quiche

Ingredients:

Pizza dough
1 Asparagus bunch
1 1/2 c. of Greek yogurt
4 Thyme leaves sprigs
3 Garlic cloves, minced
3/4 of a red onion
1 Tbsp of brown sugar
2 Tbsp of olive oil
1 c. of cheddar cheese
1/2 c. of grated Parmesan cheese
1/2 c. of Jack cheese (optional,
but if you do go with Jack,
cut the cheddar down by half)
4 eggs
Grated black pepper
Grated sea salt
White pepper

Asparagus Quiche, Cont.

Instructions:

Preheat oven to 450 degrees. It'll be enough to heat and bake this egg quiche recipe.

Cut the ends off the asparagus. You need to get rid of about an inch or so on the the ends off.

Cut the asparagus up into 2- to 3-inch spears.

Put the asparagus into a deep skillet along with some olive oil.

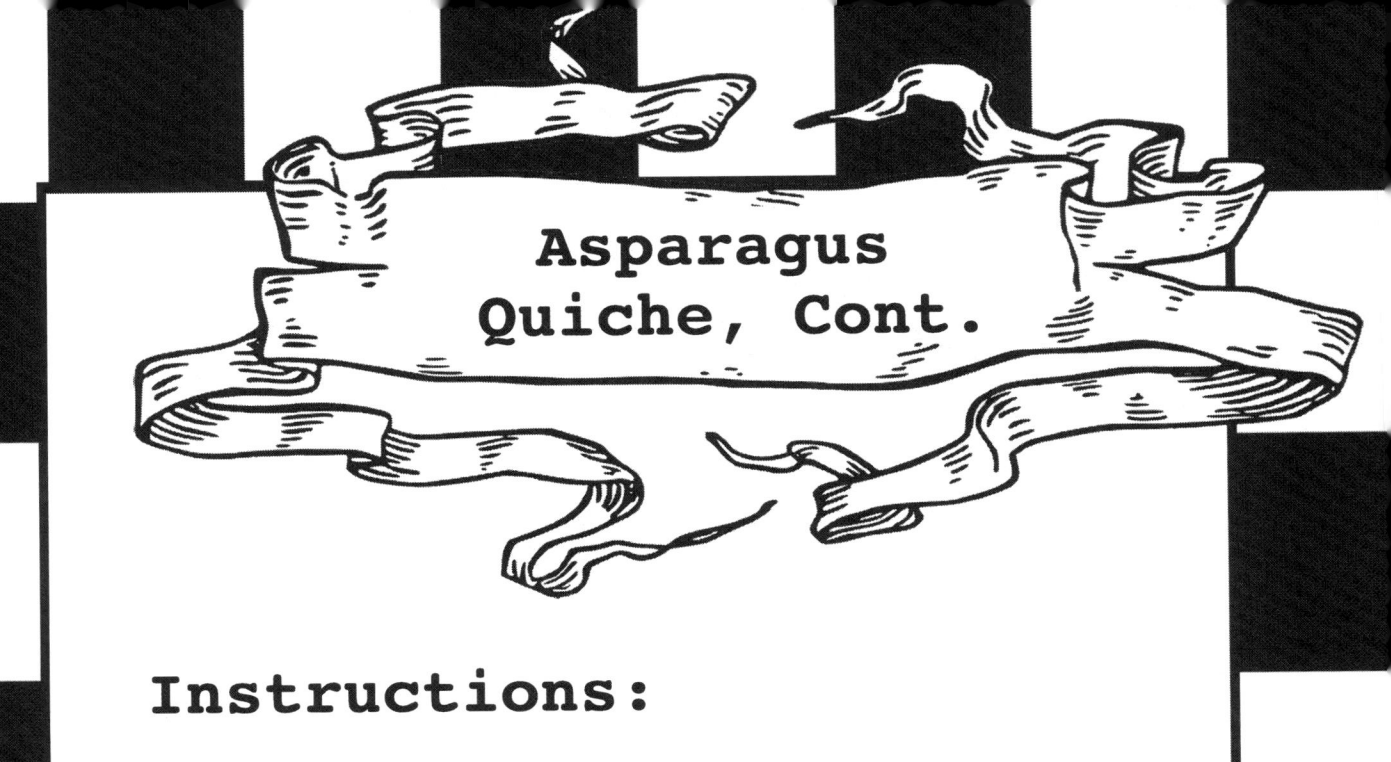

Asparagus Quiche, Cont.

Instructions:

Cook until it becomes almost tender.

Take it out of the pan.

Slice the red onion and break the sections apart.

Drop the onion slices into the pan along with the brown sugar.

Add the yogurt to a bowl.

Drop the minced garlic into the yogurt. Add in the thyme leaves. Stir the mixture up.

Add in the cheeses

Asparagus Quiche, Cont.

Instructions:

Spray the ceramic pie pan. You want to have a fairly deep pan for this asparagus quiche recipe with cheese. It'll need to accommodate the pizza dough.

Dust the bottom of the dish with some flour.

Press the pizza dough into pie pan. Dust it with some flour.

Break the eggs into a mixing bowl. Add in the yogurt mixture and the caramelized onions.

suitable for vegetarians

Asparagus Quiche, Cont.

Instructions:

Stir/ whisk together. Pour into the pizza dough pie crust. Add your seasonings. Note that the original recipe doesn't call for white pepper. It's optional, but delish.

Sprinkle the top with cheese.

Add in the asparagus spears.

Bake for a half an hour.

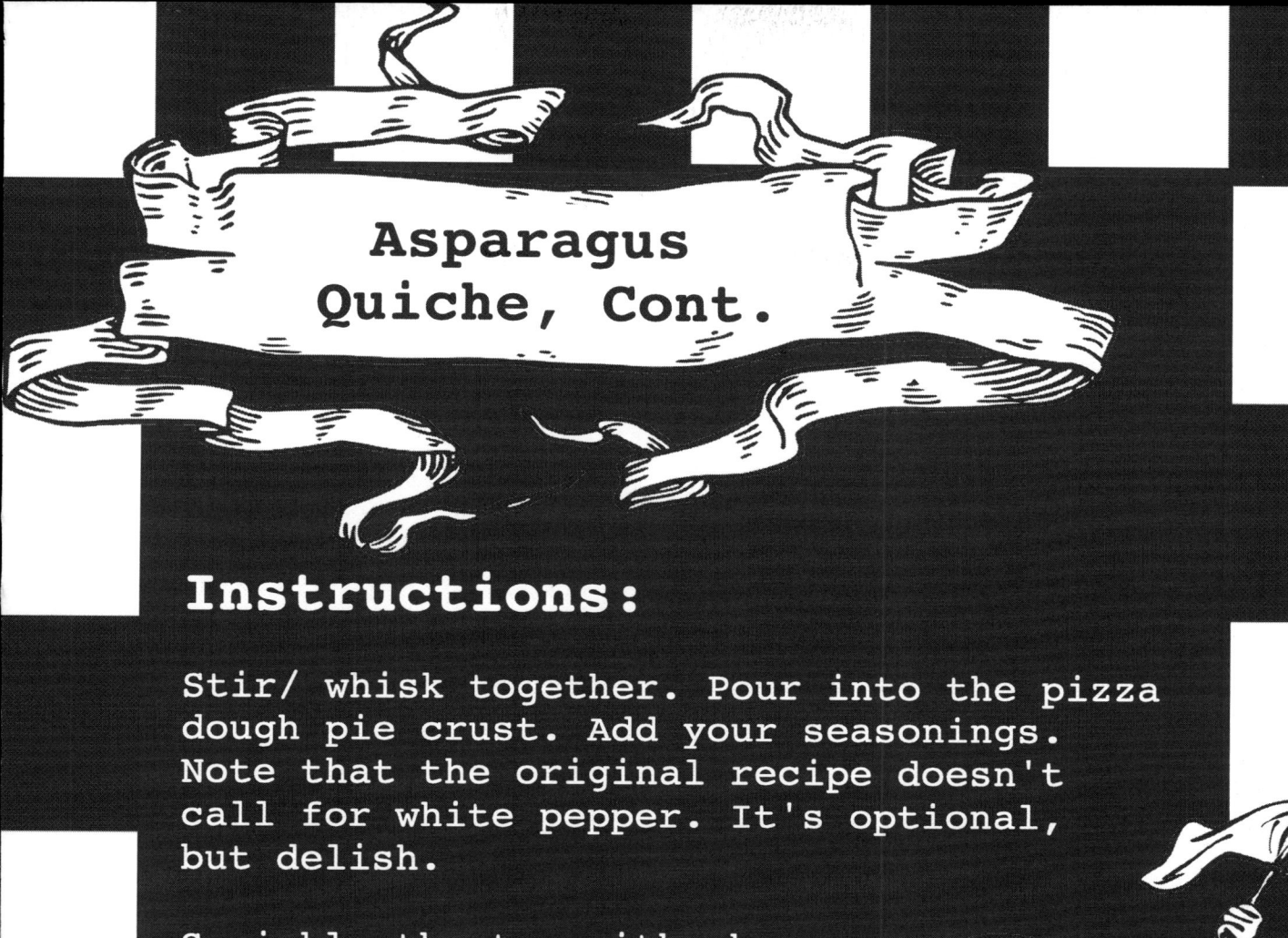

High Tea Meat Loaf

Ingredients:

1 1/2 lbs Ground beef
1 Egg
1 Chopped onion
1 c. Milk
1 c. Dried bread crumbs
2 TBSP Brown sugar
@ TBSP Dijon mustard
1/3 c. Ketchup
Dash of salt and pepper to taste
Dash of garlic powder to taste

High Tea Meatloaf, Cont.

Instructions:

Preheat the oven to 350.

Grease a 5-inch by 9-inch loaf pan.

Get out a large mixing bowl. Add in the bread crumbs, egg, milk, and beef plus the spice to taste. Put the meat mixture into the loaf pan.

Mix the ketchup and mustard plus the brown sugar in a separate bowl. Pour this over the meatloaf.

Bake it in the oven for 60 minutes.

SOMETHING SWEET SOMETHING
SOMETHING SWEET SOM
OMETHING SWE
WEET SOMETHIN
THING SWEET S
ET SOMETHING
HING SWEET SO
SOMETHING SW
NG SWEET SOME
SOMETHING SWE
SWEET SOMETH

Mmmmmm . . .

The Red Queen's Lemon Tarts

Ingredients:

1 c. Flour
1/3 c. Powdered sugar
1/2 c. Butter
5 oz. Cream cheese
1/2 c. sugar
7 TBSP Lemon Juice
4 tsp Lemon peel
2 Eggs

Optional:

Fresh raspberries or strawberries

Vanilla sugar to garnish

Did you know..."

The French word tarte can be translated to mean either pie or tart,

as both are mainly the same with the exception of a pie usually covering the filling in pastry, while flans and tarts leave it open.
...Wikipedia

The Red Queen's Lemon Tarts, Cont.

Instructions:

Preheat the oven to 425.

Prep the crust by combining flour, butter, and powdered sugar in the food processor.

Put the setting on "pulse,' and mix it until the batter forms clumps.

Place the dough in a 9-inch tart pan; Make sure you use the kind with removable sides.

Press the dough into the pan, making sure that it goes up the sides of the pan as well.

The Red Queen's Lemon Tarts, Cont.

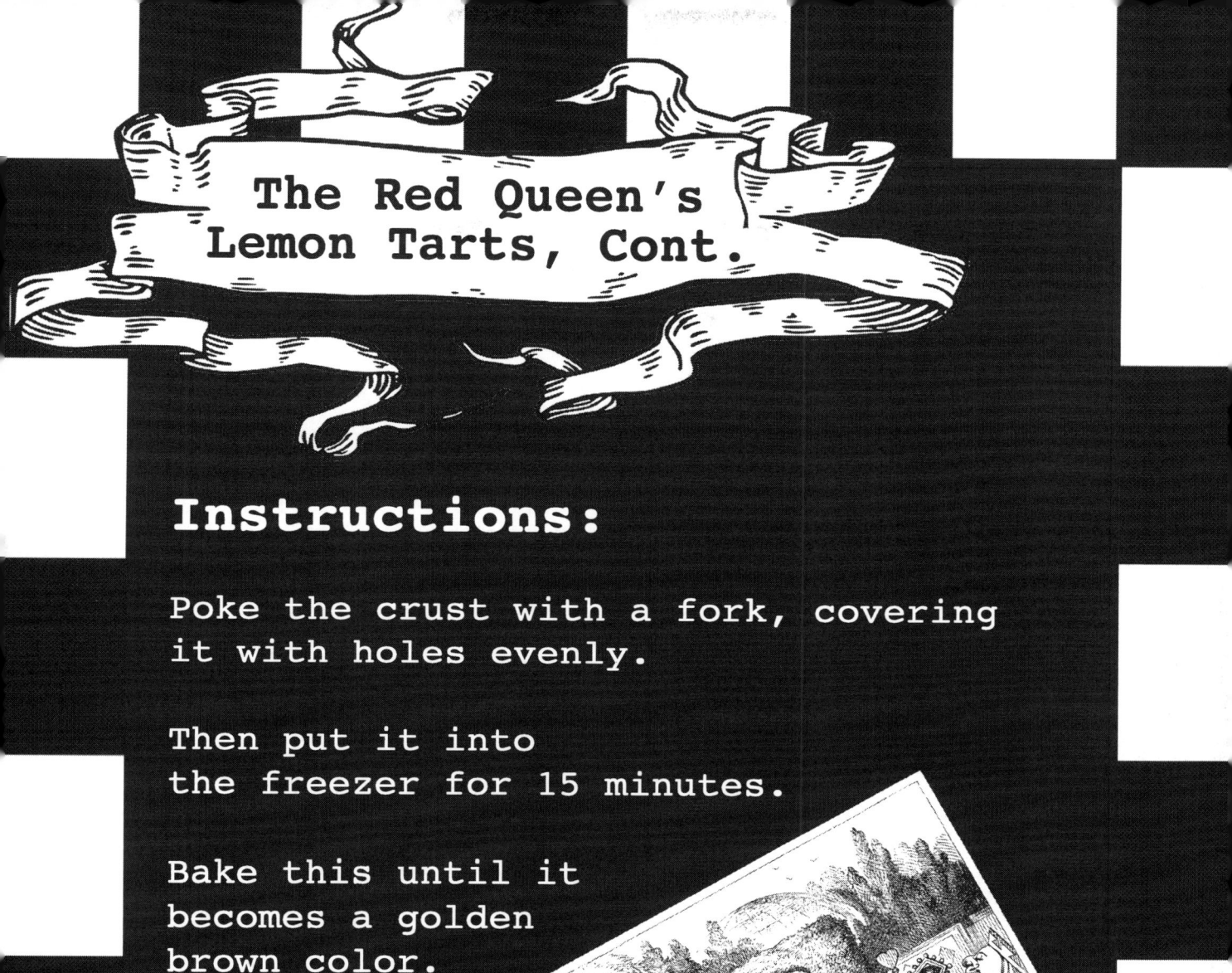

Instructions:

Poke the crust with a fork, covering it with holes evenly.

Then put it into the freezer for 15 minutes.

Bake this until it becomes a golden brown color. This should take about 15 minutes.

Allow it to cool on a rack.

The Red Queen's Lemon Tarts, Cont.

Instructions:

Turn the oven down to 350.

To prep the filling, beat the cream cheese in a bowl until it becomes smooth. After that, add in the powdered sugar, mixing this thoroughly.

Add in the eggs, beating them into the batter one at a time.

Add in the lemon juice and lemon peel. If you have fresh-squeezed lemon juice, opt for that.

The Red Queen's Lemon Tarts, Cont.

Instructions:

Pour the bater into the cooled crust.

Bake it until it sets. This will take about a half an hour.

Allow it to cool on the cooling rack again. (Cool at room temperature.)

Put it into the fridge until it becomes well chilled.

Garnish with fresh berries and sprinkle with vanilla sugar.

Waffles with Ice Cream

Ingredients:

2 c. All-purpose flour
1 tsp Salt
4 tsp Baking powder
2 TBSP White sugar
2 Eggs
1 1/2 c. Warm milk
1/3 c. Metled butter
1 tsp. Vanilla extra

Waffles with Ice Cream, Cont.

Instructions:

Preheat the waffle iron.

Mix together the sugar, salt, flour, and baking powder in a mixing bowl. Put this aside.

Get out a second bowl and beat the eggs. Stir the butter, vanilla, and milk into this.

Add the cinnamon at this stage, too.

Pour the liquid mixture into the dry mixture, and beat until it becomes thoroughly blended.

Waffles with Ice Cream, Cont.

Instructions:

Ladle the waffle batter into the waffle iron.

Cook the waffles until they look golden and feel crips.

Serve with ice cream and slices of fresh fruit like strawberries, kiwis, pineapples, and oranges.

The End

Forever Together
Coupon Book

Sample Excerpts
Forever Together

Wonderland Cafe

Date:

Time:

Notes:

Cut along the dotted line....

Pay to the order of....

1 coupon for 1 batch of homemade sweets

Date:

Time:

Notes:

Cut along the dotted line....

Pay to the order of....

1 coupon for

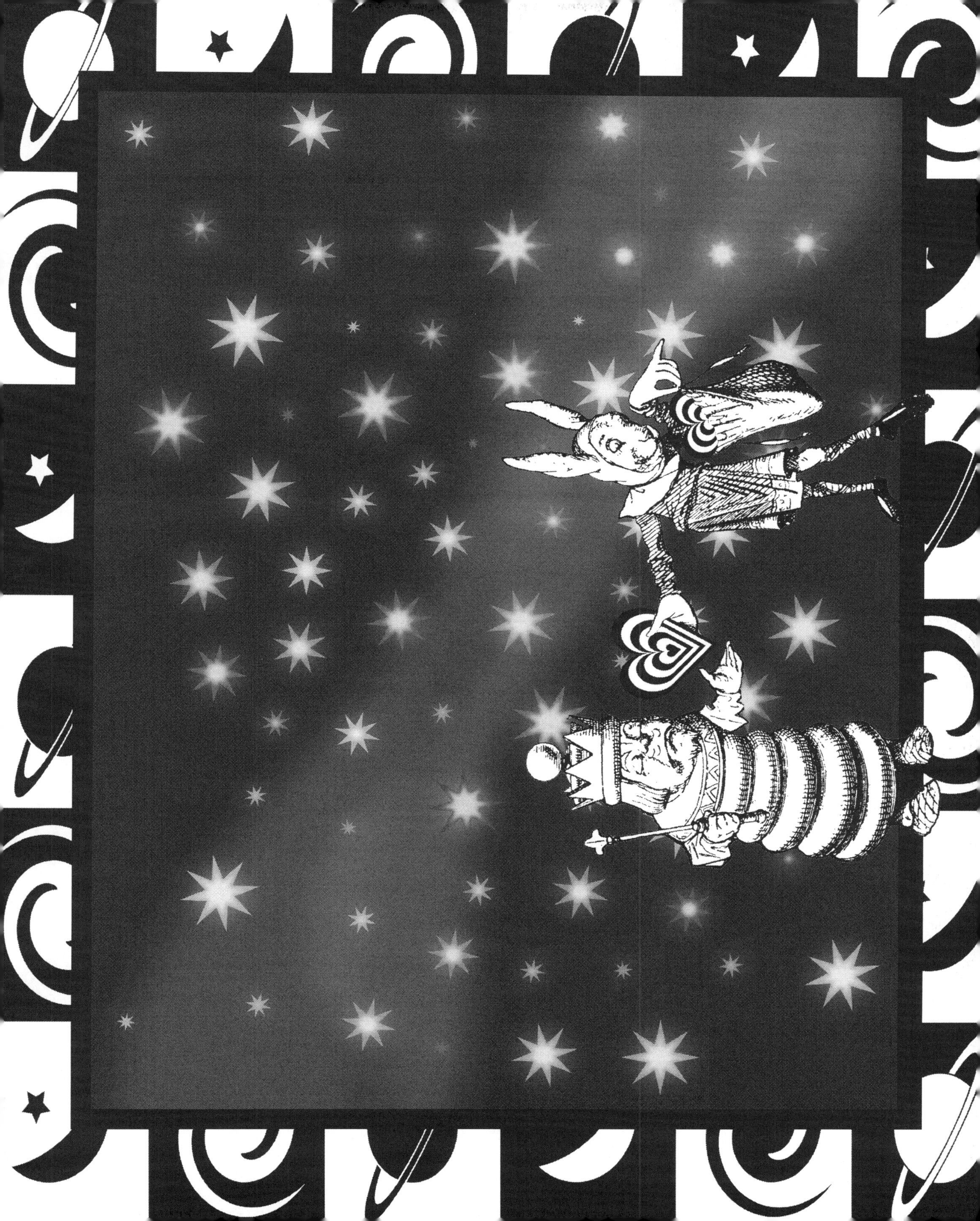

JOIN MY MAILING LIST

buffynaillonstudios.com/newsletter

Printed in Great Britain
by Amazon